Trapped in Their Script

Reclaim Your Life from Narcissistic Parents & Cultural Expectations

Agatha Peters, LCSW, LICSW

Trapped in Their Script:
Reclaim Your Life from Narcissistic Parents & Cultural Expectations

Published by Beautiful Sunshine Publishing

Every attempt has been made to properly source all quotes and attribute all research.

Interior Design & Layout: Fusion Creative Works, fusioncw.com

Paperback ISBN: 979-8-9929456-1-4
Hardcover ISBN: 979-8-9929456-0-7

Printed in the United States of America

First Edition

This book is dedicated to Nnene
who found a way to save herself

Table of Contents

Introduction

In my therapy practice, I witness the same kind of pain most days. These are empathetic, successful, even brilliant people carrying deep wounds that others can't see. It's the surgeon whose hands never shake in the operating room, but trembles when his father calls. The CEO who confidently leads board meetings, but goes silent at family gatherings. The artist whose work hangs in galleries, while her mother tells the community she's a horrible failure.

Let me tell you why this book was so hard to write. What might be difficult for most Western readers is just another way of life in many of my clients' cultures. I've sat with clients who were made to be house servants at age 8, who had an iron pressed into their skin for simple mistakes, who watched their siblings get scalding water poured on them for disobedience. These are nightmares for a lot of kids regardless of the culture, but are often overlooked in places with less resources, and I find that growing up in these cultures those resources weren't there.

In client sessions, I witnessed the devastating impact of culturally normalized abuse. I've seen people who were raped by their fathers, only to face immense familial pressure to remain silent and protect the family's honor. I've encountered mothers who broke their children's arms during so-called "discipline," with no one batting an eye. Children are beaten with hangers, shoes, and any object within reach, while elders dismiss the violence, claiming, "We all went through it."

Growing up, I often heard the adage, "Spare the rod, spoil the child," a belief that has become interwoven with intergenerational trauma and cultural practices. The brutality escalates to the point where children are beaten unconscious, yet elders continue to insist, "We all went through it," perpetuating a cycle of abuse that spans generations.

Every week, I hear stories that would shock most Americans, but in my clients' communities, these are ordinary experiences made extraordinary only because someone finally dared to speak about them.

When clients tell me about being locked in closets, starved as punishment, or watching siblings be tortured, they always add "but that's just how things were done." The community taught them that this level of abuse was simply cultural tradition. Religious leaders, family elders, and entire communities work together to maintain these patterns of harm.

This is exactly why standard therapy fails so many people from collectivist cultures. Western approaches can't grasp how deeply abuse is woven into some cultural practices. When I suggest setting boundaries to clients, they look at me like I'm crazy. Setting a boundary doesn't just mean standing up to one narcissistic parent, it means risking exile from your entire cultural identity, losing every support system you've ever known.

I wrote this book for the people sitting in my office saying "maybe I'm just too sensitive" while describing severe abuse. For those who hear "but that's our culture" every time they try to protect themselves, for anyone terrified that healing means losing their whole community: You're not alone. What happened to you wasn't okay, no matter what your culture says about it. And you don't have to choose between your cultural identity and your right to be safe.

As a Nigerian-American woman, a therapist and a social worker, I specialize in trauma, narcissistic abuse, and cultural identity, and I understand this unique agony firsthand. Every week in my practice, I sit with people trapped in scripts written by narcissistic parents—narratives that use culture to control and diminish and dismiss a person's authentic nature.

I see how these parents twist respect for elders and family loyalty into tools of manipulation. How they turn aunties and uncles into accomplices, spreading stories that paint you as the problem child, the ungrateful one, or the one who's "too

Americanized." The way entire communities stand behind them because they hold positions of cultural authority.

Clients usually find me after trying various forms of traditional therapy steeped in Western advice: "Just set boundaries." "Cut off toxic family members." "Stand up for yourself." But for the adult child of a narcissistic parent raised with collectivist values, these simplified solutions ignore the complexity of our reality.

- How do you set boundaries, when it means losing your entire community?
- How do you protect yourself, when "honoring parents" is held sacred?
- How do you heal, while staying connected to the culture that shapes your identity?

I've spent years helping people untangle cultural respect from abuse—showing them how to honor their heritage without accepting harm. In my practice, I create a space where both pain and your cultural reality can exist together. Where we can look at the scripts we've been handed and figure out which parts to keep, which to rewrite.

The impact of narcissistic abuse is profound, especially when we're taught that keeping tradition matters more than our well-being. I see clients who excel in their careers, yet carry a weight they can't name. Who build successful lives, while fighting a constant feeling that something isn't right.

In therapy, things start making sense. They realize why they can handle tough work situations, but panic at family gatherings, and why they doubt themselves despite their achievements. There's real relief in having someone understand both their pain and their cultural reality, without minimizing either one.

That's why I wrote *Trapped in Their Script*. I see too many people struggling alone with this specific type of pain, trying to make standard therapy advice work for non-Western family dynamics. When you're exhausted from years of navigating cultural narcissistic abuse, you're already exhausted enough. To heal, you need someone who gets both sides of your reality.

This book is structured in six chapters that speak directly to you, the adult child of a narcissistic parent raised with non-Western values. While the first five chapters focus on your growth and healing, the final chapter extends to mental health professionals, ensuring they provide you with culturally responsive support.

Chapter 1 brings you face-to-face with stories of others who share similar experiences. Through their narratives, you'll see how narcissistic abuse shapes lives in both unique and universal ways. Each story is different, yet the wounds they carry will feel familiar, showing you that you're not alone in this struggle.

Chapter 2 delves into the development and operation of narcissistic patterns. You'll gain a deeper understanding of the complex spectrum of narcissistic behavior, learn about its origins, and why your parent acts as they do. This explains why changing them feels impossible. Understanding their desperate need for control helps you see the bigger picture of their behavior.

Chapter 3 examines how narcissistic parents exploit cultural values and traditions for control. While many books address narcissistic abuse recovery, few explore how collectivist values complicate the path to healing and growth. This chapter is what differentiates this book from the others about narcissistic abuse recovery. Culture must be considered.

Chapter 4 helps you distinguish true narcissistic abuse from other forms of difficult behavior stemming from addictions, traumas, mood disorders, and other mental health conditions. By understanding what you're really dealing with, you can develop realistic expectations for change and adapt your responses accordingly.

Chapter 5 focuses on the ultimate goal: saving yourself. With a stronger understanding of narcissism's impact, you'll learn practical strategies for self-protection while maintaining crucial family and cultural connections. This chapter helps you to build emotional resilience, create strategic boundaries, and reclaim your power.

Chapter 6 maps out healing through culturally responsive therapeutic approaches. This chapter serves both you and the mental health professionals supporting you, ensuring your healing works within your cultural context rather than against it. You deserve support that honors both your need to heal and your cultural identity.

I wrote "Trapped in Their Script" for the child you once were, who couldn't understand why it hurt so much. For the adult you are now, still carrying those wounds while trying to balance cultural duty with personal peace. And for the self you're becoming—someone who can stay connected to their culture without staying trapped in harmful family scripts. It's never too late to reclaim both your peace and your cultural heritage from those who used it against you.

The healing starts now, and this time, you don't have to do it alone.

Chapter 1

The Wounds No One Can See

If you grew up with a narcissistic parent, you know the pain that comes with it. The anxiety that grips you when your phone lights up with their call. The dread that fills you as you step into your childhood home. In this chapter, your experiences will be mirrored and validated.

I have heard my share of horror stories as a therapist, but Chioma's experience demonstrates the ripple effect that narcissism can have in a child's life. Chioma came to my office as a Nigerian-American woman in her early thirties. More than anything, she wanted to escape the pain of having a mother who could not love her properly.

Chioma's Life with a Narcissistic Mother

Chioma's struggles began in her first adult relationship. She was only 18 when she met a man who seemed to give her everything her mother never did: attention, care, and praise. He was a doctor, who she came to find out lied about his age, saying he was 27, when he was really in his forties.

On their first date, he took her to a fancy restaurant at the Space Needle in Seattle. This was very different from the simple places she usually went. To young Chioma, who had never experienced such attention, it seemed like a fairy tale. Chioma hadn't learned how to spot the signs of a bad relationship, yet she was about to quickly learn.

Slowly, the charming doctor started controlling every part of her life, using some of the same tricks her mother had used. One of those was body shaming. Though Chioma was healthy at 140 pounds and 5'6", he criticized her weight, comparing her body to other women and watching everything she ate. He even brought his own cooking oil to restaurants and made them use it. He'd insist on driving her everywhere and picking her up.

Then, he began to hurt her physically—pushing, pinning her down, violently screaming in her face and raping her. Afterwards, he'd cry and make himself the victim. He'd use religious excuses like "the devil made me do it" to dodge accountability and make her feel guilty. Chioma, who was taught not to trust her own feelings, stayed trapped in this relationship for far too long.

But the deepest hurt came from her mother's actions. Instead of validating and protecting her daughter, Chioma's mother saw benefits for herself to this abusive relationship. She liked having a "doctor" connected to the family, and she enjoyed his attention.

When Chioma tried to leave him, her mother had an urgent and inappropriate response. "He's vulnerable. You need to break up with him slowly." Her mother even told him about Chioma's plans to leave. This left Chioma to conclude that her mom cared more about her own wants, rather than her daughter's safety.

Things got worse when Chioma had a car accident. Her brakes failed, and she later discovered the abusive doctor had damaged them. When she called her mother, scared and hurt, her mom was unmoved and acted suspicious. She believed the doctor's lies that he had nothing to do with it. To Chioma, this betrayal hurt more than any physical pain. Months later, Chioma's mother called Chioma to insist that her ex did it out of love. She said he even confessed to tampering with her car and needed Chioma to forgive him. Of course there were no apologies to Chioma for saying she had lied.

After Chioma finally escaped the relationship, her mother continued. She stayed friends with the man who had hurt Chioma. They'd talk on the phone for hours, she cooked for him, and would accept offers of his money. Years later, she even wanted him to come to Chioma's wedding, when Chioma found a kind man to marry. Her mother also tried to set up the doctor with Chioma's best friend, showing zero care for what he had done to her daughter.

The pain grew when Chioma's mother started to treat Chioma's best friend with higher importance—-letting the friend use Chioma's car and live with them for months at a time. She even asked Chioma to sleep on the couch, while her friend took the bed. Chioma found out that her mother was secretly having her ex over when Chioma's best friend was present and during Chioma's absence. Around town, Chioma's mom would call the friend her daughter and say the friend's children were her grandbabies. This crushed Chioma, causing her to feel easily replaceable.

These experiences left deep marks. More than anything, Chioma found it hard to trust herself or believe in her own thoughts. For years, she dated people who acted like her mother, because this kind of harmful love felt normal to her. Not knowing why she made these choices, Chioma blamed herself and thought there must be something inherently wrong with her.

Other people seem to be loved by their parents, and they had healthy relationships too. Chioma simply didn't know how, and it wasn't her fault. When you grow up with narcissistic parents the love is conditional, they can't love you properly. Therefore, leaving one more vulnerable to dating a narcissist who typically starts by love bombing and slowly shows their true colors later in the relationship. Clients like Chioma are much more vulnerable to this initial show of affection because they themselves are seeking love and attention that they've never received from a parent figure.

Understanding the Long-Term Effects

Having a narcissistic parent changes you. It seeps into everything: your sense of self, your relationships, the way you handle daily life, even the smallest interactions. I've seen these patterns while working with people like Chioma.

Living with a narcissistic parent teaches you to stop feeling. Every emotion you express gets shot down or used against you, so you learn to shut them off. It's basic survival. The problem runs deeper than most people realize. Once you've learned to numb yourself, it's hard to turn those feelings back on. Simple questions like "What do you want for dinner?" or "What do you like to do for fun?" become tasking or even difficult to answer.

It messes with your relationships too. Most people in your position become expert people-pleasers. You're probably the one who's always making sure everyone else is okay, taking care of their needs, and smoothing things over. You can also spot tension before it surfaces and know exactly what to say to defuse it. Meanwhile, your own needs get pushed aside because you never learned they mattered. You might not even know what they are most of the time. It's exhausting, and it never stops. There's always one more person to please, one more crisis to handle, and one more situation to smooth over.

The fear of being alone cuts to the bone. When you grow up never knowing if love will be there from one day to the next, being alone feels like drowning. That's how people end up stuck in bad relationships. Being with someone who hurts you feels safer than facing that void. The thought of leaving makes your chest tight, even when you know the relationship is wrong. The familiar pain of staying feels safer than the unknown terror of being on your own.

You might feel very protective of your personal space. That's because privacy and boundaries didn't exist with narcissistic parents. They go through your stuff, interrupt whenever they want, treat your home and thoughts as their property. That's why you might struggle to set limits with people.

- Does saying no feel impossible?
- Does having basic needs feel selfish?
- Do you overly and unnecessarily apologize?
- Does it feel awkward when your boundaries are respected?

When you grow up like this, relationships can be really challenging. Some people get clingy, desperately trying to keep others close. Some keep everyone at a distance, never letting anyone see who they really are. Some do both, pushing and pulling at anyone who tries to get close. Even typical relationship problems can feel heavy. A missed call can make you feel anxious. Having people upset with you can feel like you aren't worthy and make you feel small.

Becoming a parent yourself might carry strong feelings. Whether you're terrified of having kids because you might turn into your parents, or determined to be the perfect parent who never makes a mistake, it all comes from the same place. You've seen the damage narcissistic parents can do. The idea of repeating those patterns terrifies you. Some people spend years in therapy unlearning those patterns, before truly assessing readiness for or interest in parenthood.

Adult children of narcissistic parents are often quite successful. When you grow up with impossible standards, you learn to excel. But these wins often feel hollow. You work longer hours than anyone else. You want your work to be flawless because you're someone people rely on. But no amount of success or validation fills the hole inside. Each achievement just sets the bar higher for the next one.

All of these cause mental health impacts:

- Anxiety humming in the background
- Depression that comes and goes
- An exhausting need to be perfect
- Strict pressure to follow rules
- Haunting memories that don't go away
- Lack of trust in most people

- Deep fear of revealing your authentic self
- Suicidal thoughts just to end the pain

Isolation can be the worst part. You might withdraw because getting close to people has always meant getting hurt. But then being alone makes you feel worse, so you retreat or stay in toxic relationships. It becomes a cycle that appears difficult to break. You watch other people have normal connections and wonder what's wrong with you. Family events become something to survive rather than enjoy. Holidays fill you with dread weeks in advance.

You can change these patterns. Not through positive thinking or repeating affirmations in the mirror. You change them by seeing them clearly for what they are: The things you learned growing up as a survival technique are a form of self preservation that doesn't help anymore. By understanding and acknowledging it, we can start to build something that actually works for the life you want to have.

Yusef's Journey Through Narcissistic Abuse

While Chioma's story shows us one face of narcissistic abuse, the experience of male survivors can look different. Let me share the story of Yusef, a Nigerian-American client whose journey reveals how narcissistic abuse can take various shapes.

In the Nigerian community, Yusef's father had built himself up from nothing to become a successful businessman. To outsiders, he represented the ultimate success story. He was respected, wealthy, and influential. But inside his home, another story played out, one that left deep scars on his children, especially his sons.

The abuse followed gender lines. While his father kept certain boundaries with his daughters, he showed his sons a darker side. He would openly disrespect women in front of the boys, even "catcalling" women on the street. This sent his sons a confusing message: their sisters deserved respect, but other women did not. This double standard would later cause Yusef a great deal of confusion in his own relationships with women.

Physical abuse marked much of Yusef's childhood, and it wasn't random. His father targeted his sons with particular cruelty, using both his fists and his words. He would pit the brothers against each other, playing favorites in a way that turned natural sibling rivalry into battles that would take years to mend.

While his daughters faced their own struggles, the physical violence focused mainly on the boys.

His father's private life showed even more contradictions. While he built his business success and community standing, he kept relationships with multiple women, even underage girls. He would often abuse these women—the same women who were mothers to some of his children.

He maintained a network of victims, but in public he maintained his image as a respected community leader. He even kept a doctor on call to perform forced abortions. Some women went through this without realizing it until the abortion was completed. These are practices that, while shocking, were quietly accepted within certain powerful circles.

For Yusef, growing up with a father like this created a unique kind of pain. Like many boys, he wanted to look up to his dad and to make him proud. But how do you admire someone who hurts you and others? This question haunted Yusef well into adulthood, and the rage he carried inside felt overwhelming. Unlike many female survivors of narcissistic abuse, who rarely speak of wanting to hurt their abusive parents, Yusef had violent thoughts toward his father. These scared him, not because he would act on them, but because they showed the true depth of his pain. They revealed his true sense of helplessness.

What finally brought Yusef to therapy was fear of the future. When he noticed himself getting angry in his own relationships, he became terrified of turning into his father. This fear of perpetuating a cycle of abuse pushed him to seek help. But healing wasn't simple, especially within his cultural context.

In Nigerian culture, fathers hold a special place of honor. Questioning a father's behavior or calling it abuse can feel like betraying not just family, but the culture itself. The community's habit of protecting powerful men meant Yusef had no way to talk about his pain that felt culturally acceptable.

His anger often came out in concerning ways—punching walls, breaking things, exploding with rage in relationships. These reactions weren't random; they came from years of physical attacks, having his reality denied, and being told he wasn't good enough.

Yusef's healing came with a powerful realization: the problem was never him. No child could have been adequate enough for his narcissistic father. This opened the door for Yusef to finally feel compassion for himself, especially for his younger self who tried so hard to earn his father's love to no avail.

Yusef's story shows us that narcissistic abuse can look very different depending on gender and culture. While the pain that Chioma and Yusef carried shared some common roots, how that pain showed itself differed greatly. Understanding these differences helps us see the full picture of how narcissistic abuse affects children and families, and how the path to healing might look different for everyone.

Everyone's Struggle is Real & Profound

Chioma and Yusef's stories are just two of many examples of narcissistic abuse, but they help us understand how deeply parents can affect their children's lives. Not everyone with a narcissistic parent goes through the same lived experience that Chioma or Yusef did, but you might see parts of your own life in these stories. The pain from this kind of childhood is real and profound.

Healing starts when we accept these struggles as real. Chioma and Yusef began to get better by accepting that their pain was valid and important. Their stories teach us that no matter your culture or gender, you can break free. The most important thing to remember is that it was never your fault.

And when you see how other survivors struggle with anxiety, self-doubt, difficult relationships, and always trying to please others, you can accept your own struggles, if even temporarily, knowing they don't have to be your reality any longer.

In the next chapter, you'll learn that your narcissistic parent wasn't born like that. Like all of us, they were once innocent children too. We'll look at how early childhood experiences can shape someone to develop narcissistic behaviors. Knowing how these patterns play out helps us to soften their effects and break their cycle.

The Heart of Chapter 1

Signs You May Have a Narcissistic Parent:

- Your feelings were often dismissed or used against you
- Love felt conditional and confusing
- You learned to question your own reality
- Family gatherings create intense anxiety
- You often feel alone in a crowd of relatives

Common Ways You've Adapted:

- Becoming the perfect, problem-free child
- Disconnecting from emotions
- Isolating to feel safe
- Choosing familiar but unhealthy relationships
- Working harder than everyone else

What You Need to Know:

- Your pain and confusion make sense
- No amount of perfection would have changed your parent
- What your family called "rebellion" might have been your healthy self surviving
- Cultural respect for parents was never meant to enable abuse
- You're not alone in this experience

Chapter 2

The Truth About Narcissistic Parents

You've probably spent considerable time trying to understand how your parent became so hurtful. Like other targets of narcissistic abuse, you might have blamed yourself, thinking there must have been something you did wrong or some way you could have been different. Maria's story shows us that narcissistic parenting has nothing to do with the child and everything to do with a parent using a dysfunctional approach to getting their own needs met.

Maria's Struggle for Truth and Safety

Maria, a 45-year-old Filipino-American woman, came to my office after spending years trying to understand her mother's actions. The patterns started early. When Maria was 18, her mother pressured her to cosign for an expensive house, driven by Mrs. Santos's desperate need to prove her success in America and maintain her public image.

Soon after, Mrs. Santos invited Tito Ben, a man from their community, to live with them. Despite his meth addiction, Mrs. Santos welcomed him because having a man in the house elevated her community status. Having a male figure in the home meant more to her than prioritizing her family, and it provided a tax cut each year. To have both money and a boost of the ego was Mrs. Santos' ultimate goal.

The situation turned violent when Tito Ben became aggressive while high on meth. One evening, after eating the dinner Maria had prepared, he threatened her with a knife over a simple comment. Maria fled to the neighbors with her younger sister for safety. Making matters worse, they had young foster children under age six living in the house.

When police arrived, Mrs. Santos revealed her priorities. Instead of worrying about her children's safety, she accused Maria of "bringing shame" to their family by calling authorities on someone they called family. Her anger focused entirely on no longer having a man in the house and the potential tax money she would have received by claiming him as a household member, while her children's safety meant nothing.

From an early age, Mrs. Santos forced adult responsibilities onto Maria. By 14, Maria had become the primary caretaker for her younger siblings and cousins, managing the cooking, cleaning, and homework supervision. On top of the household work, Maria also worked full time and went to school. She was forced to hand her paycheck to her mother each payday. While her teenage years vanished under these obligations, her mother claimed credit for Maria's hard work, showcasing it as proof of her own successful parenting. Any problems, however, were distanced from Mrs. Santos's reputation.

Maria hoped motherhood might change things. Surely becoming a grandmother would soften her mother's controlling nature. Instead, it exposed ongoing patterns. When Maria briefly left her 11-month-old daughter with her mother, she returned to find the baby had been physically punished for "not sitting still," a completely normal behavior for an infant.

This incident shook Maria to the core, triggering memories from earlier in life. Her mother had always bragged about having exceptionally well-behaved children. Now, Maria understood why. They weren't naturally compliant as kids, they were terrified.

When Maria stopped allowing unsupervised visits between her mother and child, Mrs. Santos retaliated by turning the community against her. She spread stories about being unfairly "cut off" from her grandchildren, once again prioritizing her image over acknowledging her harmful actions.

"I finally realized that my mother would never be the loving Lola (grandmother) I hoped for," Maria explained. "She couldn't put anyone's needs before her own, not even a helpless baby."

In the Filipino community, where respect for parents and family harmony are foundational values, Mrs. Santos expertly wielded these cultural expectations. She maintained a polished public image, while continuing harmful behavior behind closed doors. These instances leave Maria wounded, but also wondering why her mother chooses to be this horrible towards her kids. What Maria didn't realize is, it isn't a choice, it's who she is.

How Narcissism Forms in Childhood

Stories like Maria's leave us wondering how someone becomes this way. Understanding this pattern requires looking at normal child development and where it can deviate.

While genetics plays a role, narcissistic traits can develop through childhood experiences, environment, and cultural norms. Research shows these patterns often become visible by age eight, as children learn how to relate to others and develop their sense of self.

In healthy development, babies begin recognizing they're separate from their parents around six to nine months old. Crying when a parent leaves the room shows this emerging self-awareness. By toddlerhood, between 12 and 24 months, children naturally assert their independence. But for some children, this crucial separation process becomes disrupted.

The path to narcissism can form in two ways. Some children receive excessive praise, treated as special and above criticism. This creates an impenetrable shield against failure. When these children become parents, they expect the same unquestioning adoration from their own children. Unable to see their children as separate individuals, they treat their children's lives as extensions of their own. A child's academic success becomes "proof" of their parenting skills. A child's mistake becomes a personal embarrassment.

This happens because they never learned to separate their own identity from others—first as children with their parents, and now as parents with their own children.

Another path that leads to narcissistic behaviors is when children endure severe neglect or abuse. It tells them their needs and feelings don't matter. To survive this pain, they construct a false self that feels powerful. And as parents, they desperately seek the praise and attention they were denied.

These paths (extreme praise, criticism, or neglect) create adults who struggle to feel good about themselves without constant praise from others. The ways they've learned to cope as children, either believing they're special or creating a false superior self, become deeply rooted in who they are.

This is why narcissistic patterns are so difficult to change. They aren't just bad habits that can be broken. They are the very lens through which these parents see themselves and the world.

Understanding this development helps explain narcissistic behavior without excusing it. While your parents' painful childhoods created these patterns, adults remain responsible for their actions and their impact on others.

In collective cultures there is a huge pressure to fit in (be a good, respectful child who does right by their parents and community), yet you are also expected to be the best (bring good name to your family by making someone out of yourself, even better when it comes with wealth and status). This holds true for some Asian and African communities. You are often compared to your peers and how well they are doing, and you face extra pressure to raise your kids to meet the standard of extraordinary. Parents can be extremely demanding, have a high level of discipline and be rigid, with no room for failure. In my community the statement "do you know who I am?" is often thrown around by people of status as a way to demand respect. Which in turn is saying, "I am better than you." In societies where respect is given based on wealth, people can go to the extreme to get that power.

Know the Spectrum of Behavior

Understanding narcissism becomes clearer when we see it as a spectrum, rather than a simple yes-or-no condition. Your parent might not have a formal diagnosis of Narcissistic Personality Disorder, which is actually somewhat rare, but their narcissistic traits can still cause real harm.

At one end of the spectrum, a person might show mild narcissistic traits. They might be extra sensitive to criticism or need more attention than most people. This might be frustrating to deal with, but they don't control every interaction.

Moving further along, we find people with stronger narcissistic patterns. They might struggle to feel empathy, need constant praise, or regularly manipulate others to get what they want. These behaviors get magnified when people try to correct them or set boundaries they don't like.

At the far end is Narcissistic Personality Disorder (NPD), where these traits become a fixed part of someone's personality. This is what you see in many of my stories. But please understand, they don't need to have NPD to cause narcissistic harm. Any of these characteristics and behaviors can deeply wound those around them. They have an abusive effect.

Narcissistic traits also manifest differently in different people. Some narcissistic parents are obvious about it. They brag constantly, demand attention, and clearly put themselves first. We call this "grandiose" or "overt" narcissism. Others are more subtle, showing what we call "covert" narcissism. They might act shy or humble, but still behave in self-centered ways.

The contrast between their public and private behavior is striking. Many narcissistic parents craft a perfect public image, appearing charming and generous. They often become community leaders, or excel in helping professions like healthcare and law, or become CEOs. They might rise to director positions or become respected community figures, seeming to master empathy and kindness.

But their public display of care is a performance, one they excel at maintaining. True empathy means feeling what others feel. This is what narcissistic people cannot do, even if they can convincingly act like they do.

Narcissistic Parenting Patterns

Understanding how narcissistic parents behave helps us see clear patterns in their actions. These patterns show up in how they control their children, how they handle truth, and how they respond when questioned.

1. Power Through Unpredictability

Living with a narcissistic parent often feels like walking on eggshells. You might clean the whole house perfectly, follow all their rules, and still face sudden anger or criticism. One day they might praise you for something, and the next day criticize you for the same thing. This unpredictability isn't their moodiness, it's a way to keep you off balance, so you'll keep trying harder to please them.

2. Distorting Reality

Narcissistic parents often change stories about what happened, especially when those stories make them look bad. If you try to correct them or remind them of what really happened, they become insulted or angry. They create their own version of events and expect everyone to accept it. Truth becomes whatever serves their needs at the moment.

For example, they might tell others a completely different story about a family conflict, making themselves the hero or victim.

If you point out their version isn't accurate, they might say, "That's not how I remember it," or become angry that you're "making them look bad."

3. The Illusion of Love

A narcissistic parent's expressions of love often feel empty. Their hugs might feel cold, like hugging a stranger. When they say "I love you," the words don't feel warm or genuine. This happens because real love requires vulnerability, something narcissistic people can't handle.

Their "love" comes with conditions. They might say they love you, but then list all the ways you disappoint them. Or they might only show affection when you're doing something that makes them look good. Some narcissistic parents even compete with their children, becoming jealous of their achievements or relationships. Others will show affection, but only if the child complies perfectly with their wishes.

4. Never Taking Responsibility

One of the clearest signs of narcissistic parenting is their inability to truly apologize or take responsibility for their actions. While all parents make mistakes, healthy parents can admit when they're wrong and try to make things right. Narcissistic parents almost never say "I'm sorry" sincerely. If they do apologize, it's usually to regain control, not to make amends. They have to feel superior.

5. Using Emotions as Weapons

Narcissistic parents are often highly emotional and dramatic, especially when they're confronted, or they're not getting enough attention. They might:

- Cry when you try to set boundaries
- Become angry when you don't give them enough attention
- Act deeply hurt when you make choices they don't like
- Use guilt to control your behavior
- Threaten self-harm or abandonment when they don't get their way

6. Taking Credit and Placing Blame

These parents take credit for their children's successes, but deny responsibility for any problems. If you do well in school or your career, it's because they were such good parents. They gave you the means to do well. If you struggle, it's because you didn't listen to them enough or are ungrateful for all they did.

This also shows up in how they comfort their children when they've lost or been disappointed. They point out the child's flaws and missteps, and don't provide real comfort. This is what they say is "real love."

7. The Never-Ending Needs

Narcissistic parents expect their children to constantly meet their emotional needs. They might:

- Call repeatedly throughout the day expecting immediate responses
- Demand your time and attention while giving none in return
- Expect you to drop everything when they need something
- Get upset when you put your own needs or your family's needs first

Understanding these patterns helps explain why trying to please a narcissistic parent never works in the long term. Their needs are endless, their standards keep changing, and their approval always comes with strings attached.

Recognizing these patterns helps you understand that these behavioral traits come from their own issues and upbringing, not from anything you did or didn't do. These are fixed ways of coping that they learned as a child and now inflict on their own children.

Family Dynamics Under Narcissistic Control

When a parent has narcissistic traits, they often create roles for everyone in the family. Knowing what these patterns are, once again, helps explain why your family relationships have become painful and complicated. Can you relate to these dynamics?

The Golden Child and Scapegoat Pattern

In families with multiple children, narcissistic parents often create two main roles: the golden child and the scapegoat. The golden child seems to do everything right. They are the ones to receive praise and attention. The scapegoat on the other hand gets blamed for everything that goes wrong in the family.

But the golden child suffers too. They learn quickly that their parent's love depends on perfect behavior. They live with constant pressure to maintain their position, knowing their parent's approval could vanish at any moment. Many golden children grow up with severe anxiety, always trying to be perfect.

The scapegoat faces a different set of challenges. They get blamed for issues they couldn't possibly have influenced.

- If the parent is unhappy, it's the scapegoat's fault

- If something goes wrong, the scapegoat must have caused it
- If another child misbehaves, the scapegoat must have been a bad influence

Single Child Dynamics

Even in families with one child, these patterns appear. The parent might:

- Compare their child to cousins or friends' children
- Create competition between their child and others
- Switch between treating their child as perfect and terrible
- Take other children under their wing to create artificial competition

Jealousy and Control

Narcissistic parents often become jealous when their children form close relationships with others. They might:

- Criticize their child's friends
- Try to damage their child's relationships and friendships
- Compete with their child's spouse
- Feel threatened by their child's bond with the other parent
- Get jealous of attention given to grandchildren

Extended Family Complications

Narcissistic parents often recruit other family members to support their version of reality. They might:

- Tell extended family members altered versions of events
- Turn relatives against the child who questions their behavior
- Use family gatherings to show off their "perfect" family
- Create drama at family events if they're not the center of attention

The Pain Competition

A strange pattern in these families is what we call "pain competition." The narcissistic parent must always have the worst problems or the most difficult experiences. If you're sick, they're sicker. If you're tired, they're more tired. If you face a challenge, they've faced worse.

For example, during childbirth, instead of supporting their child, they might say things like, "Well, my labor was much harder," or "Now you know what I went through." They turn even medical emergencies into competitions they must win.

Creating Teams and Divisions

Narcissistic parents often work to create divisions in the family by:

- Telling different stories to different family members

- Giving special treatment to those who agree with them
- Punishing those who question their behavior
- Creating secret alliances
- Playing siblings against each other

The complexity of these family relationships is created and maintained by your parent's need for power and importance. This helps explain why family gatherings feel so difficult and why change requires time and distance. Your narcissistic parent holds the strings in family dynamics.

Common Patterns of Control

Narcissistic parents use specific tactics to maintain power over their children. These patterns often appear in significant areas of life where they can exert the most control.

Body Image and Appearance

Many narcissistic parents use body image as a way to control their children. They might:

- Point out strangers on the street to make comparisons
- Criticize weight gain or loss, or anything they perceive as flawed about your body
- Compare siblings' bodies to create competition
- Make their own body image issues their children's problem
- Ask for constant reassurance about their own appearance
- Create no-win situations where any response leads to criticism

Special Events and Celebrations

What should be joyful celebrations often become stages for narcissistic display. During events like weddings, graduations, or religious ceremonies, narcissistic parents often:

- Take over planning to control every detail

- Invite excessive numbers of guests to create an audience
- Turn simple tasks like buying a cake into major dramas
- Make the event about themselves
- Create chaos if they're not the center of attention
- Sabotage events they can't control

For example, during their child's wedding, they might demand attention, change agreed-upon plans, or create last-minute crises. Even during their child's childbirth, they might focus more on filming for social media than offering support.

Elder Care and Guilt

As narcissistic parents age, they often use cultural expectations about elder care as tools for control. They might:

- Demand care while offering no support in return
- Use guilt with phrases like "After all I've done for you..."
- Refuse help from outside services to force family dependence
- Play siblings against each other regarding care responsibilities
- Make unreasonable demands for time and attention

The contrast becomes clear in how they handle support. They might skip their grandchildren's events, but expect everyone to drop everything when they need help.

Community Manipulation

Narcissistic parents excel at manipulating community perceptions. They often:

- Build a network of people who support their version of reality
- Create dramatic stories where they're always the victim
- Use cultural values to shame children who set boundaries
- Form relationships with vulnerable people to look caring
- Spread rumors about children who challenge them
- Turn community members into spies and messengers

They might spend years cultivating relationships with people who will do the narcissist's bidding by:

- Reporting back about their children's activities
- Pressuring children to comply with the parent's wishes
- Spreading the parent's version of events
- Making the parent look good to others

Medical Drama and Attention

Health issues become another tool for control. A narcissistic parent might:

- Exaggerate minor health problems for attention
- Dismiss or minimize their children's serious health issues

- Turn hospital visits into performances
- Use illness to demand constant care
- Compete with others' medical experiences
- Resist following medical advice that doesn't match their narrative

These tactics often increase when the parent feels they're losing control or attention. A minor procedure becomes a major drama, while their child's serious illness gets ignored or minimized.

All these patterns serve the same goal: keeping control and attention focused on the narcissistic parent. They create an environment where children must constantly manage their parent's emotions and needs, leaving little room for their own lives and growth.

In this chapter, we've explored how narcissistic parents develop their traits and why they behave in ways that can feel so confusing and hurtful to their children. You may recognize some (or many) of these behaviors in your own parent.

Remember, what matters isn't getting a perfect diagnosis or having them check every box. You're here to acknowledge the impact their behavior had on you. Nothing you did caused your parent to be this way, and nothing you could have done would have made them different.

Next, we'll move beyond typical narcissistic parenting and examine how these behaviors appear in collectivist cultures. This deeper cultural understanding will help explain why setting boundaries and seeking healing can feel especially challenging in these contexts.

The Heart of Chapter 2

How Narcissistic Parents Develop:

- Early childhood experiences shape narcissistic traits by age 8
- Some develop from too much praise, others from severe neglect
- Their own childhood wounds prevent them from seeing their children as separate
- Genetics play a role, but environment and experiences matter most
- Their coping mechanisms become permanent personality traits

Ways Narcissistic Parents Control:

- Switch between public charm and private cruelty
- Distort reality and deny your memories of events
- Use emotions as weapons to maintain control
- Take credit for successes, assign blame for failures
- Create competition and division in the family
- Turn community and family members against you

What This Means for You:

- Your parent's behavior comes from their issues, not your worth

- Their "love" feels empty because it's conditional
- No level of achievement will make them capable of real empathy
- Their need for control blocks them from genuine relationships
- Their public image often hides their private behavior
- Your experiences are valid, even if your parent doesn't fit every description

Chapter 3

Understanding Cultural Narcissism

As a therapist, I often see how cultural traditions serve as the perfect shield for narcissistic parents. They can demand complete obedience, dismiss boundaries, and control their children's lives, while appearing to simply uphold cultural values.

Jae-hoon's story shows this clearly. He came to my office at age 32, a Korean-American man trying to balance respect for his culture with protecting himself from his father's harmful behavior.

American Ways Corrupt Jae-hoon

When Jae-hoon lost his job during a mass layoff, he also hit bottom with his community. Instead of supporting him, his father, Mr. Kim, turned this private difficulty into a public shame ceremony. He invited elders to their home to criticize Jae-hoon. "You are bringing shame to all Korean-Americans," they said. "Your father left everything in Korea to give you opportunities, and this is how you repay him?" His father just nodded, enjoying their sympathy, while Jae-hoon felt crushed by guilt and indefensible.

This led to increased depression with Jae-hoon, which led his father to find another way to chastise him. He told their pastor that "American influence" was corrupting his son. The pastor said Jae-hoon just needed to return to traditional Korean values and show more respect for his elders. No one talked about his mental health or getting real help.

The situation got worse. Jae-hoon became so despondent, he had to go to the hospital after trying to hurt himself. Even this scary moment became a chance for more criticism. Community leaders came to his hospital room not to support him, but to scold him. "Do you want people to think all our children are this weak?" they asked. "This is why we need to stay true to our culture."

Even Jae-hoon's wedding to Min-seo turned into a power struggle. He and Min-seo wanted a small ceremony mixing Korean and American traditions. But his father demanded a big, expensive traditional wedding. He said this was about preserving their heritage, but it felt more like a show for the community. During the wedding, people praised his father's success in their speeches, but barely mentioned the couple getting married.

When Jae-hoon started therapy and began setting healthy boundaries with his father, the community turned against him again. Women in the community blamed his wife, Min-seo, saying she was "too American" and causing problems between father and son.

Jae-hoon's story shows a challenge many people face: how do you heal from narcissistic abuse, when your community calls that abuse "tradition?" When everyone around you says you must accept harmful behavior to be a good child, how do you find the strength to say no?

This is why we need to look carefully at how narcissistic parents use culture to control their children. Some parenting styles may seem strict in one culture, but normal in another. The problem isn't about the intensity. The problem is when parents use cultural expectations to hide their narcissistic behavior and hurt their children.

Cultural Parenting Styles

Before we dive into how narcissists use culture to hide their behavior, let's understand the basic parenting styles we see across different cultures. Think of these as tools that some parents use wisely, while others, like narcissists, can twist them to cause harm.

Four Main Parenting Styles:

1. Authoritarian: The "Because I Said So" Parent

- Strict rules, high expectations
- Kids must obey without question
- Common in many Asian, African, and Middle Eastern cultures
- Can look like: "You'll do it because I'm your parent and I said so"

2. Authoritative: The "Let's Talk About It" Parent

- Clear rules, but open to discussion
- Supportive, while maintaining boundaries
- Popular in Western cultures today
- Can look like: "Here's why this rule matters"

3. Permissive: The "Whatever You Want" Parent

- Few rules or boundaries
- Avoids conflict
- Found across all cultures
- Can look like: "Do what you what makes you happy"

4. Uninvolved: The "Figure It Out" Parent

- Disconnected from child's life
- Minimal guidance or support
- Unfortunately exists everywhere
- Can look like: "Not my problem"

What most would identify as severe abuse—beating children unconscious, causing injuries like burn marks, and forcing them into servitude—is often dismissed in collectivist cultures as discipline. This makes it harder for survivors to recognize narcissistic abuse, as extreme physical violence is just the backdrop against which their childhood played out.

This reality makes it even more crucial to distinguish between cultural parenting norms and abuse. Just because a parent is strict doesn't mean they're narcissistic. Many loving parents use authoritarian methods because that's their cultural norm.

The key difference? They soften over time.

Think of it like this: A traditionally strict Korean parent might demand perfect grades in high school, but celebrate when their adult child lands a decent job. A narcissistic parent would say that job isn't good enough. Nothing ever is.

Traditional cultural values typically are about:

- Respecting family and community
- Teaching children responsibility
- Maintaining traditions that connect generations

Narcissistic control disguised as culture looks like:

- Using tradition to demand endless sacrifice
- Never being satisfied with achievements
- Getting jealous of their child's success
- Making everything about how they look to others

Here's how you can spot the difference: Traditional authoritarian parents, even the strictest ones, usually develop a warmer relationship with their adult children. There's a point where the parent-child dynamic shifts into something more like friendship.

But narcissistic parents? They can't make this shift. They keep demanding the same blind obedience whether their child is 5 or 50. They might say "It's our culture," but really, it's about control.

Remember the narcissistic parents learned in childhood that their worth depends entirely on external validation, either through excessive praise or as a defense against severe neglect. Their compulsive need to control, rather than love, comes from desperately trying to maintain their fragile self-worth through their children's achievements and compliance.

When Culture Becomes a Shield

Many clients come to my office confused about their family dynamics. They struggle to understand if their parent's behavior comes from cultural values, personal experiences, or deeper issues. This distinction matters for healing.

Let's look at two stories that show this difference clearly:

Grace came to therapy worried her mother might be a narcissist because she needed to control everything about Grace's career. But as we explored deeper, we discovered her family's story of severe poverty after immigrating to America. Her mother's controlling behavior came from genuine fear. She didn't want her children to face the same struggles she did. Understanding this history helped Grace see her mother's actions as fear-based protection rather than self-centered control.

Song's story shows a different pattern. His father also controlled his career choices, pushing him to become a surgeon. But even after Song succeeded, nothing changed. Instead of showing pride, his father tried to compete with Song and diminish his achievements. The pattern stayed fixed, regardless of Song's success.

These stories help us see important differences between cultural parenting and narcissistic control:

In healthy cultural parenting:

- Parents can adjust their expectations while keeping cultural values
- They feel genuine joy when their children succeed, even in unexpected ways
- Their love remains steady even when their children make different choices
- They balance traditional values with their child's individual needs

Consider career expectations. Many immigrant parents push their children toward stable professions like medicine, law, or engineering. When this comes from cultural parenting, there's room for discussion and adjustment. Many of these parents might worry about different career choices, but can still support their children's decisions.

The difference, again, lies in flexibility. Cultural and fear-based patterns can shift when parents understand their children's needs. But narcissistic patterns stay rigid, no matter how much their children achieve or explain.

When Sacred Power Is a Weapon

The misuse of cultural authority is particularly devastating when narcissistic parents use spirituality against their children. In many traditional communities, religious leaders hold profound influence, their words carrying the weight of both cultural and divine authority. This makes their abuse particularly destructive, as it damages not just the child's sense of safety, but their entire spiritual foundation.

Miguel's story from Guatemala illustrates this heart-wrenching dynamic. His father served as a spiritual leader in their Maya community, performing sacred ceremonies and offering guidance to those seeking connection with the ancestral spirits. People traveled from surrounding villages to receive his wisdom, viewing him as a bridge between the physical and spiritual worlds.

But behind closed doors, Miguel's father twisted this sacred role into a tool for abuse. When he beat his son, he claimed the spirits demanded it. Even minor infractions, like Miguel's posture during meals, became opportunities for "spiritually mandated" punishment. "The spirits see your disrespect," his father would say while striking him. "They require correction."

This abuse created layers of trauma unique to spiritual manipulation. Beyond the physical pain and emotional devastation, Miguel struggled with profound spiritual confusion. How could he embrace his Maya heritage, when its spiritual practices had been used to justify his abuse? The ceremonies that should have brought him closer to his ancestors became triggers for panic attacks. The sacred spaces that should have offered comfort became sites of terror.

It took Miguel years of healing to understand that his father's actions weren't truly about spiritual guidance, but about control. With help, he learned to separate his father's distortions from the genuine spiritual traditions of his people. "I finally realized that true spiritual leaders guide with wisdom and love," Miguel shared. "They don't need to use fear or pain to teach respect."

Miguel's journey teaches us something crucial about narcissistic abuse in cultural contexts: when parents hold spiritual authority, they can make their abuse seem divinely ordained. They use their community's deepest beliefs to silence their children, making resistance feel not just disobedient, but sacrilegious. This spiritual manipulation can be extremely damaging because it attacks the very foundation of a child's cultural identity and faith.

This understanding helps us separate cultural values, which aim to protect and guide children, from narcissistic control that uses culture as a shield.

Generational Trauma vs. Narcissism

Sometimes what looks like narcissistic behavior might actually be the effects of painful experiences passed down through families. Think of generational trauma like this: when something horrific happens to a family, they find ways to protect themselves. These protective behaviors get passed down to their children, like a family recipe. But sometimes these old protective habits aren't helpful anymore.

Families might carry trauma from:

- Living through war
- Having to leave their home country
- Facing discrimination
- Experiencing poverty
- Living through hard historical events
- Losing connection to their culture

Kim's story helps us understand this clearly. She keeps her kitchen cabinets full of extra food, even though she lives near many stores and has enough money. Why? Her grandmother survived the Korean War, where finding food was very difficult. Kim's mother grew up watching her mother worry about food, and now Kim does the same thing. This isn't narcissism, it's an old survival habit passed down through generations.

Here's how trauma can travel through time:

- A grandparent lives through war and uses alcohol to cope with fear
- Their child grows up nervous, never knowing what mood to expect
- The grandchild develops anxiety, even though they never experienced war

This pattern can change when families understand where these behaviors come from. Parents who act from trauma often feel sorry when they realize they're hurting their children. They want to learn and do better.

Here's what makes generational trauma different from narcissism. Trauma patterns can change when:

- Parents learn about their family history
- They understand how past pain affects their behavior
- They see how their actions affect their children
- They want to break old patterns
- They care about their children's feelings

This helps us understand our parents better. If their difficult behavior comes from family trauma, they can learn and grow with support. If it comes from narcissism, the patterns usually stay the same no matter what changes around them.

The Community Cost of Breaking Free

In collectivist cultures, where authoritarian parenting is often the norm, "family" stretches far beyond blood relations. The community itself becomes an extension of family, creating a network where every elder is an aunt or uncle, every older neighbor a grandparent. These titles carry real weight, representing bonds that shape identity and belonging.

This interconnected bonding makes breaking free from narcissistic abuse particularly complex. As one client explained, "It's not like Western cultures where you can move to another state and start fresh. Someone from across the country might know your story, even if you've never met them." While Western authoritative parenting styles might encourage independence, collectivist communities often view separation from family as a betrayal of cultural values.

The price of setting boundaries extends far beyond losing a relationship with a narcissistic parent. It often means losing the aunties who shared their wisdom and food, the family friends who witnessed your growth, and the community spaces where you felt at home. Your cultural connections likely run through business networks, social circles, and celebrations marking the milestone in your life.

Protecting yourself from abuse doesn't mean abandoning your heritage. You can build new cultural connections that respect both tradition and personal autonomy, maintaining the valuable aspects of authoritarian culture, while leaving behind the harmful practices that enable abuse.

Yes, some community members won't understand, especially those who see strict parenting as the only path to raising successful children. They might view your boundaries as Western rebellion against traditional values. But you're not rejecting your culture by refusing to accept abuse. Instead, you're learning to preserve the beautiful parts of your heritage while recognizing when cultural expectations are being used against you.

Remember that not every strict parent is a narcissist. Some might be struggling with their own trauma, addiction, or mental health challenges, expressing their pain through the authoritarian practices they learned from their own upbringing. In our next chapter, we'll explore what else might be going on with your parent. Once again, this isn't meant to diagnose, but rather to help you choose a healing path that's realistic for all of you.

The Heart of Chapter 3

How Narcissists Exploit Cultural Authority:

- Confuses authoritarian parenting with narcissistic control
- Uses "respect for elders" to demand endless obedience
- Never allows parent-child relationship to evolve
- Becomes jealous of child's success rather than proud
- Weaponizes spiritual and community leadership
- Punishes children for adopting new cultural practices

Why Communities Often Enable Abuse:

- Collectivist values prioritize group harmony over individual needs
- Extended family systems make boundaries more complex
- Cultural stigma prevents seeking mental health support
- Community elders may enforce traditional power structures
- Fear of losing cultural connections silences victims
- Religious teachings about family loyalty get misused

The Path to Healing:

- Distinguish between cultural strictness and narcissistic control

- Recognize that healthy authoritarian parents soften over time
- Understand that true spiritual leadership guides, never harms
- Accept that setting boundaries may cost community ties
- Find others who balance cultural respect with personal boundaries
- Keep the traditions that bring joy while rejecting those that enable abuse

Chapter 4

The Difference Between Mental Health And Narcissism

When a parent's love comes with constant pain, it's natural to question the roots of their behavior. Is it narcissism or something else entirely? Many mental health struggles can disguise themselves as narcissism, making it difficult to unravel the true reasons behind the hurt.

In this chapter, we'll explore these complex layers and discover why understanding the distinctions is crucial for healing.

While my understanding is grounded in the Diagnostic and Statistical Manual of Mental Disorders (DSM-5), its approach to narcissism has limitations. The DSM-5 primarily focuses on overt narcissists—those displaying entitlement, grandiosity, a sense of superiority, and an extreme need for admiration—clinical experience and research have revealed a broader spectrum. This includes vulnerable, overt, antagonistic, malignant, and other types that aren't fully captured in the manual.

Still, the DSM-5 remains a foundational resource in therapeutic education and practice. Over the years, I've developed a more thorough understanding of narcissism through self-study, expert consultations, work with clients, and personal insights.

To better understand these concepts, let's explore Aisha's story about her father.

The Father Who Disappeared: Aisha's Story

"I used to think my father was just selfish and controlling," Aisha told me during our session, her hands trembling slightly as she spoke. "Now I don't know what to believe anymore."

Her father, Mr. Malik, had once been a pillar of his community, known for helping new immigrants find work and hosting free meals during holidays. He'd built a successful restaurant business from nothing. But five years after a car accident that left him dependent on pain medications, everything changed.

As Aisha spoke, her voice mixed with pain and confusion: "The strangest part is how he transforms. When he manages to stay clean for a few weeks, my real dad returns. He remembers every detail of my life, asks about my work with genuine interest, and truly listens. He even breaks down in tears, acknowledging the pain he's caused. But then something triggers him, and he vanishes into this cruel, manipulative person I barely recognize."

Mental health is never simple. What appears to be narcissistic behavior often masks a complex tapestry of struggles, trauma, and survival mechanisms. Before we explore specific conditions, let's understand the fundamental differences between narcissistic patterns and other mental health challenges:

- Narcissistic behavior rarely changes, even with treatment
- Other conditions often show improvement with proper care
- Narcissists maintain their patterns deliberately
- Other conditions cause involuntary symptoms
- Narcissists do not show genuine remorse
- Others often express real regret during clearer moments

When Addiction Masks True Personality

Addiction creates a unique form of emotional camouflage. Mr. Malik's behavior during active drug use showed patterns similar to narcissistic traits:

- Promising to repay borrowed money, then denying the loan ever happened
- Making elaborate family plans, only to disappear without explanation
- Dominating or completely withdrawing during family gatherings
- Turning any conversation about his behavior into accusations of his children's ingratitude

These behaviors looked exactly like narcissistic manipulation. But crucial differences emerged during his periods of sobriety:

- He could remember conversations and promises
- He showed genuine concern about his family's emotional well-being
- He could acknowledge his mistakes without defensive excuses

"Last month, he stayed clean for three weeks," Aisha shared, a hint of hope in her voice. "He came to my son's school play and sat quietly, paying attention. Later, he talked about specific moments he enjoyed. But the next week, after using again, he couldn't even remember being there."

This pattern reveals the differences between addiction and narcissistic personality disorder:

- The person's true personality emerges during sober periods
- They can feel and demonstrate real empathy when not using
- They express genuine remorse
- Their memories remain intact during sober times
- They can acknowledge causing harm without becoming defensive

Borderline Personality Disorder

Of all mental health conditions that get confused with narcissism, Borderline Personality Disorder (BPD) creates some of the most confusing patterns for families to understand. While both conditions can involve manipulation, the behaviors and motivations differ significantly.

Through my years in emergency rooms and clinical practice, I've learned to spot the key differences. Let me share an example of what this can look like. A young woman was brought in by police after causing chaos in her neighborhood—ransacking trash cans and nearly driving into yards, not because she was drunk, but because she was angry at her boyfriend. When neighbors confronted her, she escalated dramatically, threatening to get her gun. Yet when I walked into her room, she instantly switched to excessive compliments: "Oh hello darling! You look so beautiful!"

This rapid shift between extreme behaviors is what distinguishes borderline patterns. While narcissists calculate their moves carefully, borderlines act from raw emotional pain. Borderlines often:

- Create visible public chaos
- Make frequent suicide attempts for attention

- Show black and white thinking—you're either perfect or terrible
- Start relationships with excessive flattery before sudden hatred
- Get into frequent trouble with authorities
- Have multiple hospital visits for emotional crises

The manipulation looks different too:

- Narcissists plan their control tactics
- Borderlines react from overwhelming emotions
- Narcissists maintain consistent power dynamics
- Borderlines swing between extremes
- Narcissists rarely show genuine remorse
- Borderlines often feel deep regret during stable periods

In hospitals, we see borderlines "splitting" staff, meaning they make people all good and all bad. They might praise one nurse as an angel while screaming at another minutes later. They might tell different stories to care providers to create confusion. It's less calculated than narcissistic manipulation, which carefully targets specific people for specific purposes.

For children of borderline parents, the experience differs from narcissistic abuse in crucial ways:

- Unpredictable emotional storms instead of consistent control
- Intense love followed by sudden rage
- Frequent public scenes and drama
- Multiple suicide attempts as manipulation
- Genuine but unstable attempts at connection
- Deep remorse during stable periods

Unlike narcissistic personality disorder which exists on a spectrum, borderline personality disorder presents more consistently. Their challenge isn't about maintaining superiority—it's about managing overwhelming emotions that feel impossible to control.

Understanding these differences matters for healing. While narcissistic abuse requires learning to trust yourself again, borderline abuse often means learning to create stability within chaos. Both leave deep wounds, but they need different approaches to recover.

Antisocial Personality Disorder

Antisocial Personality Disorder is frequently mistaken for narcissism, but involves completely different motivations and behaviors.

- May seem self-centered
- Shows minimal concern for others' emotional experiences
- Potential for manipulative or exploitative interactions
- Characterized by a deeper disregard for social expectations

Raj thought his father Amit was a narcissist, until he started learning about Antisocial Personality Disorder. His father's behaviors followed a clear pattern: he violated others' rights without remorse, broke laws when convenient, and felt no real connection to family or social rules. When Raj spoke to his grandparents, he was informed Amit had been like that since his teenage years. He showed aggression towards his teachers and even animals. He never showed any kind of sympathy to the things he did, even destroying properties.

When Raj's sister was hospitalized, Amit didn't try to make the situation about himself like a narcissist might. He showed no reaction at all, except annoyance at having to rearrange his schedule. When questioned about his lack of concern, he responded with genuine confusion: "She has doctors. What do you want from me?"

The signs of Antisocial Personality Disorder became clearer over time. Amit regularly took money from family members without guilt, using their trust simply because it was easy. He lost jobs for stealing but never showed shame—only irritation at being caught. He started illegal side businesses, abandoned them when they became risky, and moved on to new schemes without concern for who got hurt.

"A narcissist would at least pretend to care about appearances," Raj explained. "Dad doesn't even bother with that. He sees rules and others' feelings as inconvenient obstacles to ignore. He doesn't want admiration. He just wants what he wants, and doesn't understand why anyone else matters."

Avoidant Personality Disorder

Avoidant Personality Disorder may look like narcissistic withdrawal, but stems from intense fear of criticism rather than a desire for attention or control.

- Typically withdrawn and isolated
- Driven by intense fear of criticism and rejection
- Tends to avoid social interactions
- Fundamentally different from NPD's constant need for attention

Min-ji used to think her mother's absence at important events was narcissistic behavior. Her mother missed her college graduation, her first art exhibition, even her wedding. But unlike a narcissist who withdraws to gain attention, her mother's pain was visceral.

"I found Mom crying in her car outside my wedding venue," Min-ji said. "She'd driven there, sat in the parking lot for two hours, but couldn't make herself come in. She was terrified everyone would judge her clothes, her accent, her every move."

Her mother's avoidant personality disorder showed in small ways too. She'd decline family dinners not out of disinterest, but from paralyzing fear that she'd say the wrong thing. She'd send thoughtful gifts with apologetic notes rather than deliver them in person. When she did attend events, she'd hover at the edges, looking like she wanted to disappear.

"The difference is in the motivation," Min-ji explained. "A narcissistic parent withdraws to make you chase them. My mother withdraws because she believes she'll inevitably disappoint everyone. She's not playing games. She's hiding from imagined rejection."

Obsessive-Compulsive Behaviors

Not all controlling behavior stems from a desire to dominate. Obsessive-Compulsive Disorder (OCD) presents a different narrative of control, both from deep anxiety and fear. A person with OCD seeks relief from frequent life stressors. Their actions emerge from:

- Overwhelming anxiety
- A desperate need for predictability
- Intense fear of uncertainty and potential mistakes
- Obsession, compulsion or both

Someone with OCD might:

- Take on excessive responsibilities to achieve an impossible perfection
- Create elaborate systems to manage their internal emotional chaos
- Feel intense anxiety when things deviate from their precise expectations

In stark contrast, a narcissistic individual assumes they are already perfect. They use control to maintain an illusion of superiority, while someone with OCD is constantly fighting against their own perceived inadequacies.

When Maya was young, she thought her father's controlling behavior meant he was narcissistic. Everything in their house had to follow his strict rules. Clothes had to be folded in specific ways. Homework needed to be done at exactly 4 PM. Even the cereal boxes in the kitchen had to face forward and he constantly checked that the labels were perfectly aligned. He would even check the doors at night several times before going to bed.

"I used to get so angry," Maya said. "I thought he was just trying to control us, to show he was better than everyone else."

But as she got older, Maya noticed something different. Unlike a narcissist, who believes they're always right, her father constantly worried about making mistakes. One evening, she found him redoing the family budget for the fifth time, his hands shaking. "What's wrong, Dad?" she asked. "If I make one small error, we could lose everything," he whispered. "I have to make sure it's perfect."

That's when Maya realized her father wasn't controlling their lives because he thought he was superior. He was terrified of things going wrong. When Maya got sick as a teenager, a narcissistic parent might have made it all about themselves. Instead, her father created detailed charts tracking her medicine, temperatures, and meals. Not to show off, but because he was desperately afraid of missing something important.

“The biggest difference was how he handled mistakes,” Maya explained. “A narcissistic parent usually blames others. But when my dad made a small mistake, like buying the wrong type of milk, he would blame himself harshly. He’d create new, complicated systems to make sure it never happened again.”

With therapy, Maya’s father learned to manage his OCD. His need for control came from anxiety, not a desire for power. Understanding this helped Maya see him differently—not as someone who needed to dominate, but as someone who needed help managing his fears.

Depression and Other Mood Disorders

Depression is like a heavy, persistent cloud that follows a person everywhere. Those who experience depression might:

- Appear disconnected from others
- Seem self-absorbed, when they are actually battling internal pain
- Struggle to maintain connections with family and friends
- Feel so overwhelmed that basic interactions become challenging

Kenji struggled to understand why his mother, Yumi, had changed so dramatically after his father's death. She stopped attending family gatherings, rarely returned calls, and seemed uninterested in her grandchildren's lives.

"My sister kept saying Mom was becoming narcissistic," Kenji explained. "She missed my son's fifth birthday, then my daughter's school play. When we visited, she stayed in her room. Everything seemed to be about her."

But Kenji noticed something his sister didn't. Their mother's pain wasn't performative. Unlike a narcissist who withdraws to gain attention, Yumi showed no satisfaction when family members begged for her presence. Instead, she'd cry quietly in her room, clutching old family photos.

The truth emerged when Kenji took Yumi to her doctor. She wasn't choosing to disconnect; depression had made even simple interactions feel impossible. Basic tasks like getting dressed or making phone calls required energy she didn't have.

Even with medication and therapy, Yumi's depression persists. Some days she can manage a phone call; other days, the weight is too heavy. Kenji's sister still gets angry, demanding their mother "stop being so selfish." But Kenji sees the difference. Their mother isn't choosing distance to maintain power. She's struggling to survive each day, trapped in a fog that no amount of love or anger can simply chase away.

Bipolar Disorder

Bipolar disorder creates some of the most confusing patterns for families to understand.

During manic episodes, a parent might display behaviors similar to narcissistic traits: grandiose ideas, excessive spending, demanding attention, and making everything about themselves. Then, they plunge into depression, becoming withdrawn and seemingly self-absorbed in their pain.

These mood swings create emotional environments that are both intense and unpredictable. Family members often struggle to distinguish whether they're dealing with narcissistic manipulation or the legitimate symptoms of bipolar disorder. The confusion deepens because bipolar symptoms can include:

- Periods of incredible energy and grandiosity that mimic narcissistic superiority
- Sudden crashes into deep depression
- Rapid, pressured speech about ambitious plans and complex ideas
- Impulsive decisions that could affect the whole family
- Intense irritability when others don't match their energy
- Reckless behavior that seems selfishly motivated
- Difficulty maintaining consistent emotional connections

The key difference is in the pattern itself: while narcissistic behavior remains relatively constant, bipolar disorder creates distinct episodes of mania and depression, often with periods of stability in between. Understanding this distinction becomes crucial for families trying to navigate their relationship with a bipolar parent.

Zara never knew which version of her father would show up to family events. Sometimes Abdul arrived full of grand plans and endless energy, talking rapidly about his latest business idea that would make millions. He'd promise lavish gifts, plan exotic family vacations, and speak for hours about his visionary ideas.

"During those times, he seemed like a textbook narcissist," Zara said. "He dominated every conversation, acted like he was destined for greatness, and made impulsive decisions that affected our whole family."

But unlike narcissistic behavior, these episodes would crash into periods of deep depression. The father who had been planning to buy a yacht last week now couldn't get out of bed. The difference was in the authenticity of his pain. He wasn't using these low periods to manipulate attention.

"When he's manic, Dad might spend our rent money on business schemes," Zara explained. "A narcissist would blame us for any failures or deny responsibility. But in his clearer moments,

Dad shows real remorse. He sees the damage. He just can't stop the cycle."

Zara has accepted that stability might never come. Some days she mourns the father she could have had; other days she rages at the chaos his untreated bipolar disorder creates. The hardest part is watching others dismiss him as simply selfish, missing the illness that drives his actions.

Post-Traumatic Stress Disorder (PTSD)

While a narcissistic parent controls others to feed their ego, a parent with PTSD develops controlling behaviors as survival mechanisms. Their actions stem not from a need for power, but from a brain and body still fighting past battles.

From the outside, these protective behaviors can look remarkably similar to narcissistic patterns. A parent with PTSD might:

- Demand constant updates on their children's whereabouts
- Create rigid rules about safety and security
- React with seemingly excessive anger to minor changes
- Center many family conversations around their fears
- Appear self-absorbed in their hypervigilance
- Control their environment in ways that affect everyone
- Struggle to trust others' judgment about safety

But beneath these surface similarities lie crucial differences. While narcissistic behavior stems from a need for superiority and control, PTSD behaviors emerge from a profound sense of vulnerability. The brain, having experienced serious threat, rewires itself for survival:

- Hypervigilance becomes a constant shield against perceived danger

- The need for control stems from feeling fundamentally unsafe
- Emotional distance serves as protection against further hurt
- Seemingly self-centered behavior reflects a desperate need for security
- Rigid rules attempt to create predictability in their world
- The need for validation comes from a deep wound, not entitlement
- Trust issues reflect genuine trauma, not manipulative tactics

Understanding this distinction becomes essential for families dealing with a traumatized parent. What looks like narcissistic self-absorption often masks a deeply wounded person trying to prevent further harm.

David couldn't understand why his father, a former police officer, seemed so self-absorbed after a shooting at work. His dad demanded the family follow strict "safety protocols" that seemed excessive. He forbade any social media posts about their location and schedules, and no visitors were allowed without advance notice.

"At first, I thought he was being narcissistic," David said. "He'd interrupt family events to do his security checks. He'd dominate conversations with lectures about situational awareness. If we questioned his rules, he'd shut down or explode."

But unlike narcissistic behavior, his father's actions stemmed from unprocessed trauma. During his calmer moments, he'd admit feeling ashamed of his outbursts. He didn't want attention or control. He was desperately trying to prevent another tragedy he felt he should have seen coming.

"When I started learning about PTSD, things clicked," David explained. "Dad wasn't performing trauma for attention like a narcissist might. His body and brain were stuck in survival mode, constantly scanning for threats that reminded him of that day. A narcissist would use their experiences to maintain power over others. Dad was just trying to survive each day, trapped in a loop of protecting us from dangers only he could see."

The differences became clearer in quiet moments. His father would sometimes freeze mid-sentence, his eyes fixed on something invisible to others. He'd apologize for his "paranoid" behavior, showing a self-awareness narcissists typically lack. His need for control wasn't about dominance, it was about managing his overwhelming fear that he couldn't keep his family safe.

Autism Spectrum Disorder

When working with families especially, I often see confusion between autism and narcissistic traits. Both can appear similar on the surface, particularly around social interactions and empathy, but the underlying causes are fundamentally different.

Autism affects how a person processes and understands social situations. Someone with autism typically experiences:

- Difficulty reading social cues and body language
- Challenges with making eye contact
- Problems with back-and-forth conversation
- Trouble understanding unspoken social rules
- Strong need for routine and predictability
- Deep focus on specific interests
- Discomfort with unexpected changes

The key difference lies in how empathy works. A narcissistic parent lacks empathy by choice. They understand others' feelings but choose to dismiss them. Someone with autism faces a genuine barrier to understanding emotions. They might care deeply about others but struggle to recognize and respond to emotional cues that most people process automatically.

People with autism often:

- Want to understand others better but find it confusing
- Feel genuine distress when they misread situations
- Appreciate clear, direct communication
- Prefer consistent routines and expectations
- Show authentic interest in learning social skills

This differs markedly from narcissistic behavior, where social rules are well understood but deliberately manipulated. While someone with autism might miss social cues, they rarely use this to gain power over others. Their challenges come from processing differences, not from a desire to control.

It's important to look at the patterns over time. Does the person genuinely struggle to understand social situations, but want to learn? That suggests autism. Do they understand social rules perfectly, but choose to break them for personal gain? That points more toward narcissistic patterns.

Looking Beyond the Labels

In this chapter, we've explored how various conditions can look like narcissism. Depression can make a parent seem distant. Anxiety can make them controlling. Trauma can make them appear self-focused. Addiction can appear manipulative. These are real medical conditions that need treatment.

A parent with bipolar isn't choosing to withdraw, they're struggling to function. Someone with anxiety controls things out of fear, not power. A person with PTSD acts from deep hurt, not manipulation. These differences matter because they help explain behaviors that have confused you for years.

But understanding why someone acts a certain way doesn't mean accepting harm. Whether your parent has narcissism, another condition, or both, you have the right to protect yourself. Their diagnosis explains their behavior, but doesn't excuse it.

You've spent enough time trying to understand your parent. In the next chapter, we'll focus on saving yourself. This is where you learn how to set boundaries, protect yourself, and start healing. While understanding your parent's pain is important, taking care of yourself is essential.

The Heart of Chapter 4

Signs That Mimic Narcissism:

- Addiction causing dramatic personality shifts
- OCD creating rigid control systems
- Depression leading to emotional withdrawal
- PTSD triggering overprotective behavior
- Bipolar disorder swinging between grandiosity and despair
- Borderline Personality Disorder (BPD) arousing attention
- Avoidant patterns causing consistent absence
- Antisocial traits showing genuine disregard

Key Differences from Narcissistic Behavior:

- True personality emerges during stable periods
- Shows genuine remorse when symptoms ease
- Can acknowledge harm without becoming defensive
- Demonstrates real empathy when not struggling
- Responds positively to proper treatment
- Feels authentic pain about damaged relationships
- Fear drives control, not desire for power

The Path Forward:

- Recognize symptoms can mask true personality

- Understand treatment can bring real change
- Accept that medical conditions need professional help
- Maintain boundaries while showing compassion
- Separate the illness from the person
- Protect yourself while supporting recovery
- Remember explanation isn't an excuse for harm

Chapter 5

Saving Yourself

After understanding comes action. While the previous chapters helped you recognize narcissistic patterns and distinguish them from other struggles, this chapter focuses on something equally important: saving yourself. For many adult children of narcissistic parents, this shift from understanding to action feels impossible to make alone. Years of manipulation can blur the line between normal and toxic behavior, making outside perspective crucial for breaking free.

The challenge of protecting yourself from narcissistic parents often reveals itself during a crisis. Adanna's experience shows how even simple boundaries can trigger complex family dynamics, especially when cultural expectations enter the picture.

Adanna & Kwame: Navigating Narcissistic In-Laws

The hardest moments of breaking free from narcissistic control often happen when partners witness the behavior firsthand. These incidents force families to confront painful truths that cultural expectations pressure them to ignore.

This collision of boundaries, culture, and narcissistic manipulation emerged in Adanna's story. What started with a simple bed turned into a crisis that tested both her marriage and her resolve to change generational patterns.

For weeks, Adanna's mother insisted on buying her granddaughter a bed from Facebook Marketplace. Despite Adanna and Kwame repeatedly explaining they wanted to purchase their daughter's first real bed themselves, her mother persisted. This wasn't about furniture. For the young couple, it represented their right to make decisions for their own child.

"We wanted to buy our daughter's first real bed ourselves," Adanna explained. "The crib was a gift from my aunt, not a blood relative, but you know how it is in our culture, everyone's an auntie. This bed was important to us."

While Adanna was away visiting her sister, her mother saw an opportunity. She bought the bed and arrived at their home, expecting Kwame to accept it. When he refused to let her bring it inside, what could have been a simple disagreement revealed the full scope of narcissistic tactics. Her mother began cursing at him in their native language, then escalated to threatening to call the police with false accusations of assault.

"She twisted the story completely," Adanna said, her voice trembling. "Kwame would never harm anyone. He just closed the door to keep her from forcing her way in. But my mother knows how to manipulate situations."

The incident spiraled into a barrage of phone calls to Adanna, with her mother claiming Kwame was "evil" and "didn't have her best interests at heart." This classic narcissistic strategy of dividing partners struck at the heart of their marriage.

"Kwame was devastated," Adanna shared. "He felt terrible about having to close the door on my mother, even though he knew he was right to set that boundary. He was caught between standing his ground and worrying about how this would affect our relationship."

For Adanna, the situation exposed the complex layers of her upbringing. "If I had been there, I probably would have just accepted the bed to keep the peace," she admitted. "But I realize now that would have just enabled my mother's behavior."

Through support and counseling, Adanna and Kwame learned to approach these situations as a united front. They developed strategies for setting clear boundaries while respecting cultural values, understanding that preserving culture doesn't mean accepting abuse. Their experience shows how breaking free from narcissistic control requires protecting your closest relationships from attempts to divide and manipulate.

Understanding Manipulation Tactics

Living with a narcissistic parent means constantly questioning your reality. One moment they shower you with praise, the next they tear you down completely. You might walk into a room feeling confident about a decision, only to leave wondering if you're being selfish, ungrateful, or cruel. This emotional whiplash isn't accidental. It's a calculated strategy designed to keep you off balance and under control.

While understanding their manipulation tactics won't solve any problems, it can still help you recognize when it's happening and know how to protect yourself. You learn to anchor yourself in reality, when they try to distort it. When you know their playbook, their actions become predictable, rather than confusing. Instead of being thrown off guard, you can see the manipulation for what it is.

Core Manipulation Tactics

1. The Public and Private Face

In public spaces, a narcissistic parent proudly showcases their children's achievements, telling everyone about their successes and their role in them. But behind closed doors, they unleash constant criticism about appearance, life choices, and parenting abilities. When family members hear complaints, they respond with confusion: "But they always talk about how proud they are of you!" This contrast leaves adult children questioning their own experiences, wondering if they're being too sensitive or imagining things.

2. The Emotional Warfare

A simple "no" to a family gathering unleashes a flood of contradictory messages. First come the crying emojis and claims that this rejection is "killing them with grief." Minutes later, the messages turn to rage, attacking their child's character and sense of family duty. If siblings try to help, the parent suddenly accuses all their children of plotting against them. This rapid cycling between victim and aggressor leaves you questioning your own judgment. Was saying no really that cruel? Are you the unreasonable one? This confusion is exactly what they want you to feel.

3. The Punishment and Reward Cycle

Just when you start feeling confident about setting a boundary, the manipulation begins. After refusing to let a controlling parent reorganize your home, they might disappear completely for weeks. No calls, no texts, total silence. You start wondering if you went too far. Then suddenly they appear bearing gifts and praise, acting as if nothing happened. This cycle keeps you perpetually unsteady: each attempt to stand firm triggers punishment, followed by love bombing designed to make you doubt your choices.

Love bombing happens between parent and child, though it happens more frequently in intimate relationships, as part of the cycle of abuse. It doesn't always mean lavish gifts, it can be something like flowers or jewelry, or anything they know will work for your love language. This doesn't happen randomly, it's a response to an abuse they inflicted. And their offering isn't to show love, it's meant to be a distraction and to demonstrate they're a good person. While most people would simply apologize, the narcissist finds love bombing to be quite effective because they can escape accountability and still look good.

4. The Information Twisting

Watch how a simple story changes as it travels through the family. You mention feeling tired at work, and suddenly relatives are calling to check on your "severe depression." You share a small disagreement with your spouse, and your parent spreads word of your "troubled marriage." Each experience you share gets twisted and broadcast back to you in a distorted form. Soon, you stop trusting your own experiences, wondering how they'll be used against you.

5. Digital Control and Surveillance

What starts as "parental concern" becomes a web of monitoring. They demand passwords to your accounts "in case of emergency," then use this access to track your every move. They read private emails and diaries, they record without your permission, forward your job correspondence to "help" with your career, and gather information to use later against you. When confronted, they make you question whether you're being paranoid. After all, isn't it normal for parents to want to protect their children? The worst part is, police often are unwilling and unable to help with these matters.

6. The Social Media Performance

The manipulation extends online through carefully curated photos and emotional tributes about your "special bond," making outsiders believe in their perfect parenting. Meanwhile, private messages flood your inbox, criticizing your choices and threatening to expose family secrets if you don't comply. This contrast between public praise and private criticism leaves you constantly bracing for the next attack. They may also create fake accounts so they can track you without you knowing, after you've blocked or unfollowed them.

7. The Family Surveillance Network

Restricting direct access isn't enough. They recruit others to track your life. Relatives forward screenshots of your posts. Family friends create fake accounts to follow you. Even distant relatives you've never met send friend requests, all reporting back to your parent. Each time you think you've created a safe space, another surveillance route appears, leaving you questioning who you can trust.

8. The Family Web of Control

When you set boundaries, the parent activates their network. Suddenly aunts and uncles call daily to "check on you." Your parent tells the family you're having issues. Soon, every relative pressures you to "make peace." This orchestrated concern makes you question whether you're being unreasonable. Maybe you are the problem? This doubt is exactly what they want you to feel.

9. Cultural Weaponization

The manipulation grows more complex when culture becomes a weapon. A parent might tell your entire religious community you've abandoned your heritage because you moved in with a partner. They perform public prayers for their "lost child" or spread stories about your "Western corruption." This exploitation of cultural values leaves you torn between personal boundaries and cultural belonging.

10. The Guilt Performance

Personal sacrifices become public theater. When you can't or won't meet their demands, they broadcast elaborate stories about their sacrifices for you. "I worked three jobs for your education," they announce to everyone. "Now you have success and won't even help your parent." These public performances of martyrdom make you question whether enforcing boundaries makes you ungrateful.

Know How to Protect Yourself

Physical and Digital Security

- Change passwords regularly and secure all accounts
- Keep important documents in a secure location
- Install proper locks and security measures
- Never share banking or medical information
- Create separate accounts for trusted contacts only
- Be selective about accepting new connections
- Limit what you share on public platforms

Managing Information and Relationships

- Document everything through texts, emails, and recordings
- Keep a private journal of incidents and your feelings
- Share information selectively with family members
- Have prepared responses for family pressure
- Accept that some relatives will choose sides
- Trust your own experiences and memories
- Build relationships with cultural mentors who model healthy boundaries

Building Support and Maintaining Boundaries

- Connect with others who understand your experience
- Build support systems that validate your right to boundaries
- Create clear statements about respecting both culture and boundaries
- Maintain firm boundaries regardless of their response
- Remember that genuine love doesn't require surrendering your privacy or autonomy

The Need for Deeper Healing

While protection strategies help you handle current interactions with a narcissistic parent, they don't address the profound psychological impact of growing up under their control. The damage runs deeper than most people realize, affecting everything from your sense of reality to your ability to form healthy relationships.

Growing up with a narcissistic parent often makes you doubt your own perceptions because your reality is constantly challenged or denied. Simple decisions become complicated because you've internalized your parent's criticism. Even success feels dangerous because you've learned it might trigger retaliation or guilt trips.

The psychological impact often shows up in surprising ways. You might find yourself automatically apologizing for having normal needs. In relationships, you might struggle to identify your own feelings because you spent years focused only on managing your parent's emotions. Many adult children of narcissistic parents become high achievers while privately feeling like imposters, or develop perfectionist tendencies that mask deep insecurity.

This kind of upbringing affects your nervous system too. Many survivors live in a constant state of alertness, unconsciously bracing for the next criticism or manipulation attempt. Your body remembers the pattern of walking on eggshells, even when you're in safe relationships. This physiological impact can manifest as chronic anxiety, sleep problems, or unexplained health issues. It can even trigger a mental health disorder.

Cultural expectations often compound this trauma. In many communities, family loyalty is considered sacred, making it harder to acknowledge parental abuse. The pressure to maintain family harmony can trap you in harmful patterns, especially when cultural or religious leaders emphasize forgiveness without accountability. These cultural binds create additional layers of shame and confusion that need specific attention in healing.

The Reality of Ongoing Contact

Sometimes completely cutting ties isn't possible or desirable. Cultural obligations, shared family connections, or practical necessities might require maintaining some level of contact with a narcissistic parent. This reality demands a different kind of protection: emotional armor that lets you engage when needed while keeping your core self safe.

Think of emotional armor as an invisible shield. It's not about being cold or cruel, but about protecting your inner self, while navigating necessary interactions. This means keeping conversations superficial, sharing minimal personal information, and having prepared responses ready for common triggers. It requires you to make a distinction between what is shared and what must be kept protected behind the shield.

Consider what happens during required family gatherings. Your parent might probe for personal information or try to create drama. With emotional armor in place, you can politely deflect invasive questions or calmly excuse yourself from heated situations. You remain present physically while keeping your emotional self protected.

Narcissistic parents rarely let go completely, even when their children try to distance themselves. They need their children for specific purposes:

- As living proof of their "excellent" parenting
- For practical help or financial support
- To maintain control over the family narrative
- As a source of attention and drama

When you know why they're maintaining contact, you can better prepare for their attempts to pull you back in. It's important to control what information you feed to a narcissistic parent. This means being selective about what you share.

Never share details about:

- New relationships until they're well established
- Work achievements that could trigger competition
- Personal struggles they might use against you
- Future plans they might try to control
- Financial information they don't need to know

Recovery requires a complete reprogramming of your survival instincts. The hypervigilance that protected you as a child now prevents you from relaxing into healthy relationships. The people-pleasing that kept you safe now stops you from advocating for your needs. The emotional detachment that numbed the pain now blocks genuine connection.

Finding the right professional support becomes crucial because this healing work requires guided practice in a safe environment. Unlike standard therapy approaches, recovery from narcissistic abuse often requires specialized understanding of both trauma and family dynamics. A skilled therapist can help you reconnect with your authentic self while developing practical skills for managing ongoing family contact.

Breaking Free Is a Process

This chapter shows how recognition leads to action. Once you understand narcissistic manipulation tactics, you can finally protect yourself from them. The parent who once left you questioning your sanity now follows patterns you can name and anticipate. Their attempts to distort your reality lose power once you see them clearly. And as Adanna and Kwambe's story demonstrates, sometimes maintaining limited contact becomes necessary, requiring both practical strategies and emotional armor.

Understanding brings power, but saving yourself often requires outside, professional support. The final chapter guides therapists and counselors in providing this crucial help, showing them how to navigate both the psychological impact of narcissistic abuse and the cultural complexities that surround it.

The Heart of Chapter 5

First Steps to Freedom:

- Learn to spot manipulation tactics early
- Create specific protection strategies
- Build support systems outside the family
- Secure your privacy and personal information
- Document patterns of control and abuse
- Trust your own experiences and perceptions

Protecting Your Core Self:

- Develop emotional armor for necessary contact
- Control what information you share
- Navigate cultural pressures without surrendering
- Maintain boundaries despite backlash
- Keep your closest relationships safe from interference
- Find balance between respect and self-protection

The Path Forward:

- Accept that saving yourself takes priority
- Understand that healing requires outside support
- Know that freedom might mean limited contact
- Remember you're breaking generational patterns
- Recognize your right to protect yourself
- Trust that peace exists beyond their control

Chapter 6

Cultural Pathways to Healing

I've sat on both sides of the therapy couch. As a Nigerian-American, I remember sitting in my therapist's office listening to advice that ignored everything about my life. "Just limit contact," they said, not understanding how my church, my extended family, and my entire support system was connected to the person hurting me. Their advice made me feel more alone than ever.

Now, as a therapist, I see this same pain in my clients' eyes. They come to me after trying other therapists who couldn't understand their world. A Chinese client told me about a therapist who kept pushing her to move out of her parents' house, ignoring that living with family was normal in her culture. A Nigerian man described how his previous therapist called his family "dysfunctional," missing that being the eldest son meant responsibilities he couldn't just walk away from.

These stories keep repeating. Clients from Indian, Latino, and other minority communities tell me about therapists who know about narcissistic parents, but can't understand why "just cutting ties" isn't possible. They don't see how culture affects everything about healing.

The Community Corrects Anjali

Anjali's story shows exactly what typical therapy misses. When she came to my office, she'd already tried three different therapists. Each one helped her identify her mother's narcissistic behaviors, but they couldn't help her handle the other challenges she faced.

The breaking point came during her birthday celebration. Anjali had carefully planned every detail, trying to balance what she wanted with what her culture expected. Then, a community elder called about her mother's invitation to the party. "Did you send a proper invitation? When did you invite her? Why didn't you follow our traditions?"

The questions sent Anjali into a panic attack. Her previous therapists might have seen this as simple anxiety, but it showed a bigger problem. Her mother had spent years building relationships with community elders who now watched Anjali's every move. Even a birthday party had to follow strict rules, or the community would step in to correct her.

At the party, her mother showed exactly how she used culture to control Anjali. She timed her arrival when other community elders were present, making sure everyone saw her acting like a perfect mother. The birthday card she brought exposed the manipulation that happened behind closed doors. While traditional birthday cards from mothers usually express love and wishes for happiness, her mother simply wrote that she had given Anjali her beauty, and there was nothing more she could give her. She signed it with just her name—-no "Love, Mom" or warm wishes. It was a power move disguised as a gift, reminding everyone that Anjali's beauty came from her, while also declaring she had no obligation to give maternal love.

This moment helped Anjali see how her mother's control worked through the entire community. It wasn't just about their relationship anymore. Her mother used cultural expectations and family honor to maintain power. Regular therapy that only focuses on setting boundaries misses how deep this problem goes.

Creating Therapy That Actually Works

Standard therapy often fails people from different cultures because it assumes everyone can heal the same way. But healing from narcissistic abuse requires understanding how each person's culture affects their experience. Let me share what I've learned works better.

Understanding Thoughts and Beliefs

Cognitive Behavioral Therapy (CBT) helps people recognize harmful thinking patterns created by narcissistic abuse. But we need to adjust it for different cultures. Instead of just challenging negative thoughts, we must explore how cultural beliefs about family, respect, and communication affect these patterns. For someone raised to believe that questioning parents is always wrong, we need different tools than standard CBT provides.

Looking at Family Patterns

Traditional therapy often digs into childhood experiences to understand current problems. This still matters, but through a cultural lens. We must examine how family dynamics were shaped by cultural expectations, immigration experiences, and community pressures. What looks like control in one culture might be normal protection in another. We need to understand these differences without excusing real abuse.

Using Mind-Body Healing

Many cultures have their own traditions for healing trauma. While Western therapy might suggest meditation or breathing exercises, these aren't always the best fit. Sometimes traditional healing practices, spiritual rituals, or cultural ceremonies provide better paths to recovery. We must incorporate whatever methods resonate with each person's cultural background.

Building Trust and Understanding

When someone comes from a culture that values family loyalty above all, they need to know their experiences are believed. This means making space for both their pain and their cultural reality. Many clients have spent years being told to accept abuse as normal or that setting boundaries means betraying their culture. Having someone validate their experience while respecting their cultural identity makes a crucial difference.

Creating Lasting Change

Real healing happens when therapy addresses both personal safety and cultural truth. Take financial abuse, for example. When a client struggles with giving their entire paycheck to abusive parents, we don't just say "stop giving them money." Instead, we explore what financial support means in their culture, find ways to maintain appropriate help without enabling abuse, and work through the guilt that comes with setting limits.

Sometimes this means having hard conversations about which cultural practices to keep and which to question. A Latino client taught me about the deep commitment to family above all else. Instead of telling him to reject this value, we worked on redefining it. He found ways to redefine what being a good son meant while still protecting his own family from his mother's manipulation.

Finding Community Support

Most importantly, therapy needs to help people find others who understand their experience. Group support often works better when it brings together people from similar cultural backgrounds who face the same challenges. They can share strategies for handling community pressure, maintaining cultural connections, and finding freedom without losing their roots.

Approaching Clients and Setting Boundaries

When working with clients from diverse cultural backgrounds, it's crucial to approach the topic of narcissistic abuse with sensitivity and awareness. Failing to do this can make it incredibly difficult for clients to acknowledge or confront abusive behavior from their parents.

As therapists, our role is to create a safe space where clients can explore their experiences without fear of judgment or pressure. This means:

1. Asking about their experiences rather than immediately labeling their parents as narcissists. Let them share their stories and validate their feelings before introducing clinical terminology.
2. Acknowledging the cultural pressures they face. Recognize that setting boundaries or speaking out against parents can feel like a betrayal of cultural values.
3. Helping them understand that setting boundaries is not disrespectful. Rather it is a way of honoring their own needs and well-being, which is essential for healthy relationships.
4. Exploring ways to maintain necessary family connections while still protecting their mental health. This might

involve setting limited, specific boundaries rather than cutting off contact entirely.

When it comes to actually setting boundaries, it's important to remember that this is a learned skill. For survivors of narcissistic abuse, it can be particularly challenging because they've been conditioned to prioritize their parents' needs over their own.

Here are some key principles to share with clients:

1. Keep boundaries simple, clear, and specific. For example, "I can talk on the phone for 10 minutes once a week" rather than "I need more space."
2. Be prepared for pushback or resistance. Narcissistic parents often see boundaries as a challenge to their authority. Help clients anticipate and plan for these reactions.
3. Set consequences and follow through. If a boundary is violated, there need to be clear, consistent consequences. This might mean ending a conversation, leaving a situation, or limiting future interactions.
4. Recognize that it's a process. Setting and maintaining boundaries takes practice and may need to be adjusted over time. Celebrate each step as a victory.

Throughout this process, it's essential to validate the cultural complexities clients are navigating. They may feel guilty, ashamed, or conflicted about setting boundaries with their parents. Normalize these feelings and affirm their right to protect their own well-being.

Instead of pushing clients to make dramatic breaks, we focus on small, sustainable changes. A Chinese client learned to say "I'll think about it" instead of giving an immediate yes to her mother's demands. A South Asian man started taking longer to answer his father's calls rather than picking up on the first ring. These seemingly tiny shifts help build confidence for bigger changes.

The key is teaching boundary-setting as a skill that honors both culture and self-protection:

- Start with boundaries that don't challenge major cultural values
- Practice responses that feel culturally appropriate
- Prepare for community pressure and backlash
- Find ways to show respect while maintaining limits
- Build support systems that understand both worlds

Building Support That Understands

Traditional support resources often miss what people from different cultures need. They focus on individualistic solutions without considering how community ties affect healing. We need support systems that grasp both the abuse and the cultural pressures surrounding it.

Finding Cultural Mentors

Look for healthy elders in your community who model boundary-setting while maintaining cultural connections. They can share wisdom about navigating family expectations without sacrificing self-respect. Their example proves you can honor culture while protecting yourself.

Creating Safe Spaces

Some clients find healing in groups specifically for people from their cultural background dealing with narcissistic parents. These spaces allow them to share struggles without having to explain cultural context. A group of South Asian women might understand immediately why moving out of their parents' home feels impossible, while a general support group might not grasp these pressures.

Building Professional Networks

Having culturally aware professionals makes a huge difference. This includes:

- Therapists who understand your cultural reality
- Religious leaders who support healthy boundaries
- Legal advisors who grasp family obligations
- Financial counselors who understand family money dynamics
- Friends who support you without you having to constantly explain your trauma

Establishing Emergency Support

Many people stay in abusive situations because cultural pressure limits their options. Having practical support ready can make boundary-setting possible:

- Friends who can offer temporary housing without judgment
- Work colleagues who understand sudden family emergencies
- Community members who won't report back to family
- Resources that respect cultural dietary or religious needs

Healing Without Hiding Your Culture

Working with survivors of narcissistic abuse taught me something crucial: healing has to make sense in your own cultural world. I've watched too many clients struggle with well-meaning but culturally blind therapy. They sit in offices being told to "set boundaries" when their whole community considers that disrespectful. They hear about "self-care" when their religion teaches that suffering brings growth.

But I've also seen what works. When therapy creates space for both the pain and the cultural reality, real healing happens. One client found strength in her traditional prayers, turning them from obligations into moments of peace. Another kept his role as eldest son while learning to protect himself from manipulation. They didn't have to reject their culture to get better.

This changes everything about how therapy works. We stop pushing Western ideas of healing and start listening to what matters in each person's world. Sometimes that means working with religious leaders who understand healthy boundaries. Sometimes it means finding support groups where everyone gets why you can't just move out of your parents' house.

Most importantly, it means understanding that safety and culture can exist together. You can keep the traditions that give your life meaning while letting go of the ones that hurt you. You can find ways to honor family without accepting abuse. You can build a life that makes sense in your world.

For therapists, this isn't just about learning different cultures. It's about really getting how culture shapes everything—the abuse, the healing, and the whole path forward. Every client brings their own cultural truth into the room. Our job is to help them find freedom within that truth.

The Heart of Chapter 6

What Therapists Need to Know:

- Standard therapy fails when it ignores cultural reality
- Family obligations often can't be severed
- Cultural identity matters as much as individual healing
- Every culture has its own ways of healing
- Encouraging small changes and meeting the client where they are at is honoring a client's autonomy towards their healing journey

What Actually Works in Therapy:

- Adapt therapy to fit cultural frameworks
- Work with community leaders who understand boundaries
- Find healing in cultural practices, not just Western methods
- Help clients navigate community pressure
- Create support groups with shared cultural understanding

Building Real Change:

- Start with changes that honor cultural values
- Help clients protect themselves without losing their roots

- Cultural practices can be a strength
- Create safety plans that make sense culturally
- Show how boundaries and respect can coexist

Conclusion

To the Courageous Souls Rewriting Your Story,

When you first opened this book, you took a powerful step towards liberation. You chose to face the pain of narcissistic abuse head-on and confront the cultural expectations that have kept you caged. As a woman who has navigated these complexities myself, I want you to know that I see you, I believe in you, and I'm proud of you.

Rewriting the script that's been forced upon you is no small feat. It requires unlearning decades of conditioning and daring to define your own path forward. It means setting boundaries with the very people who raised you and learning to trust your own voice over the chorus of critics in your head. It's a daily practice of choosing yourself, even when every fiber of your being has been trained to put others first.

But here's the thing: you're not starting from scratch. By reaching the end of this book, you've already begun the rewriting process. You've gained invaluable tools and insights that will serve you moving forward. You've started to recognize the patterns that have held you back and envision a life that truly belongs to you.

As you continue on this path, remember the wisdom of our ancestors. They knew that healing is not a solo endeavor, but a communal one. Surround yourself with people who affirm your worth and remind you of who you are beneath the roles you've been forced to play. Seek out spaces, both in person and online, where you can show up fully and authentically. Let the strength of your community fuel your own.

Remember, too, that rewriting your story is an act of generational healing. By breaking free from the cycles of abuse and oppression, you're not only saving yourself—you're paving the way for a new legacy. You're showing the child within and the generations to come that a different way is possible. That we can honor our culture without being shackled by it. That we can love deeply without losing ourselves.

As you continue rewriting your script, know that setbacks and stumbles are inevitable. There will be days when the old patterns feel inescapable, when the voices of guilt and shame grow deafening. In those moments, return to this book. Reread the passages you've underlined and the notes you've scribbled in the margins. Reconnect with the parts of you that feel most alive and untamed. Trust that you already possess everything you need to create a story that sets you free.

Because the truth is, you are your own best healer, teacher, and advocate. You are the expert of your own experience. And you are the author of your own liberation.

So keep rewriting. Keep choosing yourself, day after day, with the tenacity and audacity of those who came before us. Keep daring to imagine a life beyond the limitations you've been handed.

Your story has the power to shift generations and reshape culture itself. The world needs your healing, your truth, and especially your unbridled joy.

I'm right beside you, believing in you every step of the way.

Keep rewriting,

Agatha

Acknowledgments

To Kate Davis: When I think of the best therapists, I think of you. You continue to be my inspiration in this field.

To Aunt Molly: You've been my rock since I was a teenager. Your strength and support came exactly when I needed them most.

To my husband, Udim: Thank you for always being an anchor.

Author Bio

A licensed therapist with years of experience in emergency room crisis intervention, Agatha Peters specializes in helping people find their way back from depression and suicidal thoughts. Drawing from her expertise in CBT and EMDR therapy, she has guided countless clients toward healing and renewed purpose. Originally from Nigeria and now based in the United States, she brings a unique multicultural perspective to her practice. Her debut book, "Trapped in Their Script," helps adult children of narcissistic parents navigate healing, while honoring their cultural heritage.

www.ingramcontent.com/pod-product-compliance
Lightning Source LLC
LaVergne TN
LVHW101441200926
848483LV00001B/12
* 9 7 9 8 9 9 2 9 4 5 6 0 7 *